DEVELOPING MENTAL POWER

MAXWELL PRESS

DEVELOPING MENTAL POWER

George Malcolm Stratton

Professor of Psychology in the University of California

MAXWELL PRESS

Chennai Trichy NewDelhi

MAXWELL PRESS

This edition has been published in india by arrangement with Carson Books, UK

ISBN 978-93-90063-65-9 Maxwell Press

No. 44, Nallathambi Street,
Triplicane, Chennai 600 005

MJP 910

Publisher : C. Janarthanan

Publisher's Note

The legacy of a country is in its varied cultural heritage, historical literature, developments in the field of economy and science. The top nations in the world are competing in the field of science, economy and literature. This vast legacy has to be conserved and documented so that it can be bestowed to the future generation. The knowledge of this legacy is slowly getting perished in the present generation due to lack of documentation.

Keeping this in mind, the concern with retrospective acquiring of rare books has been accented recently by the burgeoning reprint industry. Maxwell Press is gratified to retrieve the rare collections with a view to bring back those books that were landmarks in their time.

In this effort, a series of rare books would be republished under the banner, "Maxwell Press". The books in the reprint series have been carefully selected for their contemporary usefulness as well as their historical importance within the intellectual. We reconstruct the book with slight enhancements made for better presentation, without affecting the contents of the original edition.

Most of the works selected for republishing covers a huge range of subjects, from history to anthropology. We believe this reprint edition will be a service to the numerous researchers and practitioners active in this fascinating field. We allow readers to experience the wonder of peering into a scholarly work of the highest order and seminal significance.

MAXWELL PRESS

NOTE

A PART of what is here offered has appeared in an article called "The Mind as Misrepresented to Teachers." The author wishes to thank the Editor of the *Atlantic Monthly*, where the paper was first published, for permission to reprint it. In preparing the present monograph, however, the earlier paper has been entirely rewritten and new material has been added.

CONTENTS

EDITOR'S INTRODUCTION

EVERY teacher requires a working knowledge of the fundamental nature of the human mind. Without it teaching cannot be made either an interesting or a creative occupation. When psychologically uninformed, the teacher can operate on the mind of youth only in a formal and mechanical way, applying traditional and contemporaneous methods of procedure without much ability to adapt technique to conditions for the purpose of gaining predictable results.

Certainly the teacher who would make his teaching life an interesting and effective adventure with youth will wish to possess whatever scientific insight is necessary to an artful stimulation and control of growing minds. We recognize the field of human psychology as vast. At best its mastery is a patient and difficult matter. The important thing is to make a correct beginning. It will be highly economical of energy and discouragement. The waste of wrong views and partial views can hardly be overestimated. And such waste is largely avoidable if only the first general view of the nature of mind is accurately acquired. Fundamental truths gained and held in a comprehensive way will be a continuing source of critical and constructive suggestion, a constant safeguard against error, a persisting guide to the accurate interpretation of new facts and theories of mind prolifically offered in an age deeply interested in psychological truth.

We have long sought a presentation which would give teachers and other daily workers with mind a simple general view of mental life in its fundamental working aspects. We have been fortunate enough to find the exposition required, and it is offered in this monograph. We are confident of the influence it will have upon the American public which reads books on psychology. We are especially glad to offer this statement of the theory of the developing mind in a series intended for teachers because of the particular form of argument which the author has utilized to express his views. It meets with beneficent directness most of the fundamental doubts and controversies which have enmeshed the teaching profession for a quarter of a century.

For a long time the managers of school organizations, the makers of curricula, and the supervisors of teaching processes have been divided as to which particular theory of mind they should follow in the settling of their practical educational affairs. Should they follow the general faculty psychologists, hallowed by a long tradition, and say that the subjects of study are not of primary importance, inasmuch as certain large functions of the mind, such as memory, imagination, reasoning, etc., may be trained in almost any subject because the power gained will transfer? If so, then only a few subjects need to be included within the curriculum, and the traditional courses with a well-established technique will obviate the waste of mastering new subjects and the methods of teaching them. Or should they follow the special disciplinarians, taking sanction from recent scientific evidences, and say that the mind is so highly and finely differentiated and specialized that the only way to be sure of a wholly disciplined mind is to give it training through as large a variation of special experience as it is possible for the school to give? If so, then subjects or contents are of prime importance, the curriculum must contain many subjects instead of a few, new as well as old.

Each side of the controversy has summoned respectable scientific evidence to support its particular point of view, and by interpretation minimized the significance of the opposing facts. Gradually there has been an abandonment of extreme claims on both sides, but for all the scuttling of arguments, two points of view have remained to confuse the layman and the teacher. In the case of the educationalist it has meant continuing confusion, dualism, and indecision in educational practice.

It is therefore not difficult to understand the warm appreciation which experienced and thoughtful teachers will have for a theory of mind which will settle controversial matters in a way that is obedient to the sum total of science and consistent with the faiths created by long experience, supply missing considerations which a purely intellectual interpretation of mind has ignored, and give that unity of view which will make the application of psychology to the problems of mental development, at least in fundamental matters, a consistent matter free of the controversies and confusions, the compromises and the indecisions of the last two or three decades. It is with the greatest assurance that we predict the influence of this small volume. Teachers everywhere should read and discuss it. Then the most fundamental controversy which has harassed the profession will cease to exact most of its toll of wasted argument and lop-sided action.

DEVELOPING MENTAL POWER

I

IS THE MIND A GYMNASIUM OR A TOOL-CHEST?

IF we can see, though in outline, what the mind is, much that is dark both to parent and to teacher begins to clear. One may now know in what quarter there is hope of success, and where failure, and may set his course accordingly. Decision as to the general character of the mind is thus momentous; it almost of itself writes down one's educational creed.

Yet upon the very outline of the mind the doctors disagree. Science is brought to the support of opposite assertions, and the layman, bewildered, knows hardly where to look for guidance. Perhaps for a short time we shall do well if we merely sit by, listening to the contention, knowing that it is of weight for practice and is no mere pleasant play of wits; knowing that we cannot, as teachers and parents, avoid decision and must heed the disputants so that our conclusion may be more wise than theirs.

DEVELOPING MENTAL POWER

The child's mind, says the one contending group, is a union of a few powers or faculties — like attention, observation, memory, imagination, and reason. And such powers it is the teacher's duty to render strong and supple by well-chosen exercises, found, some have held, in subjects such as mathematics or the classic languages. These great mental powers, once they become vigorous and elastic, stand ready throughout life for all important needs. Nor does it greatly matter whether the subjects studied have intrinsic value; the weighty thing is that they should discipline the mind. Reasoning, for instance, is of such value that time is well given to its cultivation even by a study such as geometry, a knowledge of which may never in itself be of any practical good. The particular kinds of knowledge needed for one's life-work, it is held, cannot be foreseen, depending so largely on later circumstance and choice. But by a mind disciplined this knowledge will readily be gained when the need itself is clear.

Schooling so planned need not be with an eye wholly averted from the useful; there may be heed first of all to the most useful of things, namely, the mind itself, training it well in the beginning and expecting it thus to meet, in true economy, the demands of whatever later is the work in hand. Schoolmen who hold to this belief purpose that the mind's powers shall be given strength and full activity; and that, if this work be well done, the person will meet the later need not only of buying and selling, of medicine and law, but also of the still wider service and enjoyment which is not a matter of bargain and sale.

But now for a moment their opponents shall have the floor. And these impatiently declare that all who believe in a few great mental powers and would direct the school to their discipline are suckled in a creed outworn. Science has destroyed the simple faith. Experiments by James, Thorndike, Woodworth, and others have shown how idle is the attempt to train these general powers; have shown, indeed, that there are no general powers to train. The belief in such powers goes with the antiquated idea of mental faculties, now of merely historic interest and swept aside with phrenology and its absurd map of the skull and brain. No study gives general training; it gives only particular training. James, for example, carefully noted the time required for him to learn a certain number of lines of Victor Hugo's *Satyr* and then for more than a month "trained" himself memorizing the entire first book of *Paradise Lost*. On going back to learn a new portion of Victor Hugo's work of exactly the length of the old, how much evidence did he find of a memory strengthened by its month or more of exercise? No evidence; he had to give more time than before to the task. Likewise Thorndike and Woodworth, who practiced the estimation of the area of rectangles, found that a marked improvement with rectangles of a given shape and size brought no like improvement with rectangles of another shape and size. And it has been observed that neatness attained in arithmetic papers brought no slightest neatness in papers of language and spelling.

Having destroyed in this way the faith in general powers and their training, what do the destroyers offer in its place? A belief in particulars and in particulars only. Instead of a single power of memory, there is a power to recall colors, another power to recall sounds; and so on, we know not how far. The mind, this group maintains, is our convenient name for countless special operations or functions. We may train one of these functions or a number of them, but not a faculty in general — attention in general, or observation in general, or reasoning. Further, these countless particular functions are independent; they act almost as though they were insulated from one another; when you have trained one of them, you have trained that limited function and none else. What you do to the mind by way of education knows its place; it never spreads. You train what you train.

The educational corollary of this latter belief is of wide effect. It means that we must discover the specific reactions, the specific information, which the child will use in after life and make sure that he possesses these and only these. If life will not demand of him the particular knowledge, the particular functions used in algebra, the study of algebra is time wasted. If in life he will find application for the special ideas, the special reactions involved in chemistry, time spent upon chemistry is well spent. The teacher's direction of attention here veers from east to west. At the center of interest is no longer the child's mind, but the particular situations in life which the child, become man, will have to face. Of a study we are to ask, "Does it contribute to the doing of the things that later will have to be done?" and not, "Does the study make the child's mind more alert, or sound, or sane?" "The purpose for which subjects are taught," writes Dr. Abraham Flexner, "lies not in the pupil's mind, but in the subject-matter and its relation to existence and life." Dr. Ernest C. Moore, who speaks with vigor at this point, holds that "when we teach we do not make minds or strengthen minds or draw them out." Instead of giving to the mind form, we give it information. Instead of moulding the mind, we are to fill the mind. Where the education whose aim is mental discipline might have as its symbol a stripped athlete busied with Indian clubs and chest weights for strength and agility, the education which opposes mental discipline and calls for mental contents might have as its symbol some receptacle that is being filled — a tool-chest, with screw-driver, chisel, and plane.

II

DEFECTS IN THE RIVAL ACCOUNTS

THE controversy is thus in brief before us, each side with its different account of the mind. "Believe the psychologist," cries a recent writer to the schoolmen. And this encourages one to examine these two descriptions, and judge them by our present scientific knowledge. It may well be that neither can be accepted; that in their place there must be a picture of the mind markedly different from either and with a far richer promise for education. Even in opposing these rival accounts a truer outline of the mind will, I believe, appear.

Surely the mind is ill-described by most believers in mental discipline. In so far as our remembering is explained by a faculty of memory, and our reasoning by a faculty of reason, we are offered mere words in the place of causes. But along with explanations that do not explain are clear errors. The mind is divided into great powers — like sight, hearing, memory, imagination, reason — each of which is supposed to be almost simple and uniform throughout. And this we know is false. Memory is not a simple thing, but involves many kinds of acts, several of which are no more important for remembering than for seeing, imagining, or reasoning. Again, if by reason we mean syllogizing, it is not one of our principal powers; and if we mean by it the ability to think and act reasonably, this comes only from a fine conspiring of almost every power we have.

Moreover, the believers in mental discipline too often fix their interest upon the powers by which we know, our intellectual faculties, and treat like a stepmother those great powers by which we take delight and are moved to passion and make resolve and act. Not only do large matters thus suffer neglect, but in consequence the very spring and strength of our intellectual powers themselves are ill-understood. The sources of judgment are not seen nor the conditions of its success. A certain deftness of bare intellect is overvalued, to the misprising of the deep forces that drive and direct the intellect, as well as of something more nearly external, the definite and detailed knowledge of the objects with which intelligence must deal.

The defects of this account of mind are thus

greater than many even of its critics seem to know. But some of the defects are caught and well denounced by those who hold the mind but as a receptacle to be given "contents." They rightly see the mind helpless even were it deft and strong, they see its lack of actual knowledge. They see also that the mind is of immeasurably more varied powers than are nominated in the short list of faculties in which the old schoolmaster was taught to believe.

But with these rugged virtues why not take the whole doctrine of "contents" to our hearts?

First and perhaps least important, its watchword confirms the ignorant in their ignorance. We are only too ready to regard the child's mind as a vessel into which knowledge is to be poured, and the new doctrine would appear to give to this crude notion a scientific seal. So far as the child's training is viewed as mental contents, the mind itself is viewed as a receptacle, a container. And a container is both inert and indifferent. A tool-chest takes no active part to receive its tools, and a sharp chisel is to it no better than a rusty broken one. Merely glance at the metaphor and its absurdity is revealed depth on depth. Those who believe in mental contents would cry out with one voice that they did not mean *that.*

For if there is anything upon which psychologists are agreed, it is that the mind is active; not indifferent but selective, forever choosing and rejecting. Even its humblest experiences, the colors and sounds by which the world is known, are not "given" us, but are the mind's unique and mysterious response to external stimulation. Hue and tone, as we directly experience them, the students of physics and psychology are agreed, do not exist in the external world. They are our reaction; and with them we create for ourselves a strange counterpart of the reality without. And for one object awakening enough interest to be noticed, ten have vainly assailed our eyes and ears and been ignored. These acts of notice and selection do not seem acts, being without effort, without strain of will. But action is not always marked by effort: a child at play is as active as a child at some deadening task.

If the things we see and hear enter the mind hardly as into a passive receptacle, more clearly is this true of our recollections, our imaginings, our conclusions reasoned out. Unless we actively reconstruct the past and recognize it as past, we do not remember. The child can possess no imaginings or judgments save what he has himself imagined or judged. Nor can he create them once, and forever after "contain" them; each time that they are before him they must be created afresh — on the instant, usually, and with no slightest hint that power has gone into their remaking. As well call the ever-new movements of some graceful dancer the "contents" of her body as use this name for the marvelous expressions of the mind.

And still more clearly is this dead image broken by the will. In his purpose the boy proclaims himself no mere recipient, but a doer; not clay, but the potter. He takes his place among the infant deities, imposing his ideas upon brute substance until in some measure it is made into the likeness of his mind.

But we waste time upon this unhappy watchword of the party. Not until we find a tool-chest that helps to fashion and use the tools it holds, a tool-chest that is also both machinist and carpenter — not until then will this image do more than darken counsel.

Turning now from metaphor to plain statement, let us ask whether it be true that practice keeps its place, that you train only what you train. It would be of startling, and, to some, almost disheartening, importance if the child's improvement in a foreign language — French or Latin, let us say — had no effect upon his command of the English language, or upon his interest in European history.

The experiments in clear support of this doctrine, however — that you train merely what you train — are few; most experiments contradict it. Improvement in judging the area of certain figures, as was just said, does not bring equal improvement in judging other figures. But the judgment of these other figures is not left untouched. On the contrary, it receives marked benefit. And while neatness in classroom may remain within narrow limits, it can easily be made to pass these limits. If the children in writing their arithmetic lesson, for example, are urged to neatness as of universal value, their papers in geography also will be neater, even though this other subject may not be named in the urging. Or, again, if a person practice with the right hand the tossing and catching of balls, keeping two in the air at once, until he has attained a high degree of skill, will the effect of the practice be confined to the right hand? No; it will appear also in the left; it may be as though fully two thirds of the practice had in some way been transferred to the hand that has not been practiced at all. And in many other directions of research, transfer of training is found. The cultivation of the mind is thus not at all like that of land, where the ploughing of one field does not affect the soil beyond the fence. Effects here do not stay confined, but spread.

It will hardly be possible to follow the attempted explanation of this spread; it can hardly be explained away. Nor need the teacher feel dismayed because the improvement in one study — let us say physics — is not transferred entire to all other forms of acquisition; that some of the good is lost in transit. Even a spread of small amount, as Thorndike has said, may be important; the effort would be well repaid if practice in justness of conduct in school were to bring even the slightest increase in justice of conduct in all other relations of life; or if his accuracy in work at school make him even a little more accurate in all ways when he has left school.

Instead, then, of proving that you train what you train, the psychological experiments which have so troubled the waters of education prove that normally you train what you do not train. Indeed, these experiments seem to have been seized upon by men convinced already and beating about for evidence, rather than by men unbiased and glad to go wherever the evidence might lead.

But the question just considered, Whether the benefits of training can be transferred to regions that have not been the immediate place of the training? is intimately connected with another. Indeed, we shall find this other but an aspect of the problem of transfer. But to it we must attend if we would judge aright the position of the partisans of "contents."

Is it then true, as some maintain, that our mental powers are stubbornly particular and never general in their character? Is it, for example, absurd to think that there can be a habit of punctuality, in accordance with which the child, and later the man, may practice promptness in keeping all manner of appointments? Or must we think that such a habit must be mere promptness at school, and promptness in no wider kind of conduct? Taken rigorously such a contention would seem to mean that there could be no punctuality for school in general, but only for the particular school, for the particular room in the school, for — but one must not press too far.

From some assertions that are heard one might think that a mental function is something good for little more than a single narrow situation, like the special bow that can be used only upon presentation at court. Let us, to test the truth of this, take almost an extreme case.

Even so particular a response, so particular a habit, as that of answering the telephone is far less particular than it seems; it is run through and through with generality. It is called forth in many different situations; varied, too, is the action called forth. What you respond to is never quite the same: now it is a loud ring near by, and now a tinkle in the distance; now it is the clear note of a bell, now it is the whirr of a "buzzer." And your response is never the same: you arise, take a few steps and stand at the instrument; or again, you remain seated and bring the instrument to you; you speak with deference, you speak with impatience, you speak with a martyr's resignation. Never quite the same signal, never quite the same movements of the body, never the same words spoken, never in the same tone, never to the same purpose.

If one cannot but see the breadth and openness in even so restricted a habit as this, how much more general are the significant forms of action which the schools can rightly have at heart. The child who is inclined to "give up" at the least difficulty has a habit which applies to many and most varied situations. And if, instead, he can be turned about, can be made to assume a fighting attitude toward what is hard to do, he has been brought to attain what is applicable in ten thousand times and places. The attitude of credulity, of helpless acceptance of whatever is stoutly asserted, is almost universal in little children. Nor is it a trait which is called forth only in some few and special situations; but rather upon all those infinitely varied occasions when persons meet and speak. And in its stead there can be the habit which means that one will hesitate, will weigh and test, will look to the evidence for all important statements. Likewise the child's impulse to look first and foremost to his own particular self — to be vain, to be selfish, to sulk — this is a general form of action which displays itself in endless variety of detail and place. And no less general is the change from all this, so that he begins to see the interest of others and to let this be a constant check upon his self-seeking, a spur to action that is generous.

These habits of mind, and a host like them, are perhaps less wide than the memory-in-general or the reason-in-general of the older education. The question whether the only appropriate term for them is "particular" or "general" would have delighted the professors of old Padua or Bologna. For us the important thing is to see their immense range of use, in all manner of situations and by all manner of men, whether they be day-laborers or diplomatists.

Considered with care, then, we can heartily accept neither the description in which the mind is made to be a composite of a few great faculties, nor that in which the mind appears as an endless array of distinct functions. We have discerned something of what is wrong in these accounts.

III

THE INTERPLAY OF MIND AND BODY

EVEN in what has been reviewed thus far, we have caught glimpses of the mind's behavior. But there has been interest in refutation, in denial; and denial by itself profits little. Perhaps this spirit of contention can now be quieted, to become the prelude of something positive and favoring, and we shall be willing to look directly at the mind itself, to see, if possible, its constitution. When once we have ceased to notice our disputants save upon occasion and out of the corner of the eye, their artificial divisions of the mind into faculty and function will in due time tone down to their proper value. The reality of the mind will gradually be restored to us; even, as in looking at the picture of the dissected muscles of the face, we can in time correct their true and yet false impression, knowing that these ghastly members are in life fed with warm blood and clothed in soft skin and controlled by affection and intelligence, and in their stead we see once more the human and expressive countenance.

And first of all we shall see that the mind with all its variety of operation is one, is organized, is whole. Its powers may be distinguished and named and discussed separately, but they hold together; no one of them can be understood, much less trained and educated, apart from its fellows.

Indeed, the mind itself is vitally connected with the body, and the child is both mind and body. Whatever seriously influences his body influences his mind. If he is mentally slow or is widely uninterested, we may well inquire whether he is undernourished or physically fatigued, or in bodily discomfort, or is sick. Poisons uneliminated that disturb the child's nerves and muscles disturb also his mind; they poison his intelligence, his emotions, his will. Some of the great discouragements of teaching will be gone when, by wise coöperation with the home and with physicians and nurses, these conditions in the bodies of school-children are everywhere recognized and are given the care which science would suggest. Deafness, defects of sight, may be at the bottom of what seems utter lack of interest. The child's sense of vigor, of well-being, which makes him ready to push on through difficulties; or that opposite condition, in which he is listless or discouraged or irritable — these are often the expression of the bodily state, and are weakened or made more intense, according to the direction in which the bodily state is changed.

Even the muscular "set" of the face reacts upon the mind. A child will more easily be cheerful deep within, if his sour expression can even artificially be sweetened. A sullen look if forced to become a smile is apt to start a change which leavens all his feeling until the smile is free and genuine. Likewise the position of the body affects the attitude toward the object of our attention. A child will notice the difference, if first he undertake his problem with body all languid and ill-supported, and now he pull his body together, making it energetic, even aggressive, toward the task in hand.

That the body, if ill-treated, will take vengeance upon the mind may be illustrated in another way. It is not safe even for the health and progress of the mind to interfere with what seems so unmental a function as that of right-handedness or left-handedness. A left-handed child, if he be compelled continuously to suppress his preference and to act as though he were right-handed, will in some cases show symptoms that are a clear fusion of bodily and mental distress. He may come to stutter and, becoming embarrassed, may incline to remain alone. The original violation of that which, according to our present knowledge, is an innate advantage of one side of the body, has here disturbed the delicate nervous mechanism of speech and, through that, has changed the color of distant regions of the mind; and relief has been known to come when the interference ceased. We are only at the threshold of our knowledge of the brain and of the interrelations of brain and mind. It is improbable that a serious effect in one part of the brain-cortex ever leaves the rest of the brain-cortex, or leaves all forms of mental action, unaffected. The change may be greater in one region than in another, but it is perhaps never narrowly circumscribed.

But while the body thus influences the mind, the reverse is also true. The eagerness of the child's interest is reflected in his kindly look, his forward-bent body; his boredom, his vacant eye, his fidgeting. But in a less passing way the mental condition is all the while helping to build or tear down the body's strength and health. The digestion of food, the rate and depth of breathing, the action of the heart and of the other parts of the system that carries the blood — all these and more are constantly being spurred or reined in — because of what goes on in the mind.

Healthful interests, healthful enjoyment, freedom from worry, are strength-giving for the mind and body of children as of adults. The effect of emulation in school, that within bounds is so wholesome; the hunger for the praise, the dread of the blame, of teacher and parent; — these are rightly kept short of persistent anxiety, especially in the weak and the sensitive. Moreover, certain forms of skill found in professional work would be impossible without strong support from consciousness. A dentist whom I know is of the opinion that the young men among his fellow students who had character have become the more skillful dentists; those of weaker stuff did not drive themselves on, but rested with inferior work; that the one man in a large city who he knew had the greatest reputation for skill had carried through and then taken out the same piece of work six times before he could himself be satisfied with it. How much more is the creative skill of hand of the great sculptors, painters, and musicians connected with extraordinary powers of mind, and not of body only.

Yet one might easily from all this expect a more precise accord between certain bodily and mental functions than is actually found: it has not been proved, for example, that success in manual training points to success in such studies as English, mathematics, or science; those that have unusual skill of muscular movement do not, as a class, appear to be the ones that have high intellectual ability. It would seem, then, that although we can well expect large mental benefits from whatever makes the body well-knit and resistant to disease, yet we can prophesy less surely for the mind from those physical activities that include some particular precision and skill, and which are found to occur, not infrequently, without full strength and health of the body entire. But in spite of these particular exceptions, it has been found by Mead that normal children as a group are heavier, taller, and stronger of body than are feeble-minded children. And Doll showed that even within a group of defective children there is a relation between their bodily and their mental measurements: as we go down the scale of mental defects, we come to greater physical defects as well. Thus we find reciprocity between mind and body; currents of cause and effect run back and forth between them, bringing consciousness and the nervous system with all the other physical organs into an intercourse that is constant, uniting them to make the person one and complete.

IV

INFLUENCES WITHIN INTELLIGENCE

PASSING from these evidences that the bodily and the mental functions interplay, let us now observe to what extent the mind's own functions touch one another.

We shall see the need, first of all, of *knowledge.* If one is to think effectively of sugar beets or airplane engines, he must study such beets, such engines. But he will not think effectively upon these if he think of these alone; his interest and his knowledge must widen to the principles of agriculture or of aerodynamics; and beyond, he will need botany or physics, and chemistry. Chemistry, then, is important for a lad uncertain whether he will deal with beets or engines. But what of the boy who does not himself know, and whom no one as yet can tell, whether beets, engines, taxation, tuberculosis, or the Gospel will lie at the center of his thinking in the time to come? Must he give laborious years to all of these and to a thousand things beside, that he may be ready for the day of action? Inevitable and enormous waste is in that direction. He had best be at home in the central studies into which all special subjects lead. These more central studies may be less attractive just because they are more abstract, more remote from some particular work in hand; and for that reason more of art may be needed to make the "practical" youth, hating abstractions, ready to give himself heartily to their forbidding generalities. The skill of the teacher is displayed in conquests of this kind. General truths, when seen and understood, are so much more powerful instruments than are mere particular and detached bits of knowledge, that surrender upon this point will hardly be permitted by any able teacher. Most children prefer to play with an electro-magnet than to ascend from this to the principles of electro-magnetism; prefer to look at striking chemical reactions than to attack with vigor the general truths involved; prefer to draw circles and polygons than to understand geometry. The interest in these general truths is, in a sense, less natural, more a matter of civilization, and has to be imposed upon the child by a kind of contagious interest felt by another who can see the endless applications of what is universal. One has to fortify himself with the stern conviction of this, in order to resist those who see only the attractiveness of an endless list of particular studies of nature and of handicraft and who would urge them to such a pitch that there is no firm grasp of the sciences which deal with principles. Particular and general ideas conjoined is our need; errors of practice are thus avoided; economy of action is reached. Judd found, in striking at a target under water where refraction had to be allowed for, that those who were instructed in the principles of refraction had the advantage over those who merely kept at their interesting target practice without instruction. And in the experiments upon neatness it will be remembered that the neatness spread to other work when there was presented the general idea of neatness and of its value as a universal trait. Ideas, then, are guides, are directors of habit; in them is compacted wisdom, and whoever tries to do without a good stock of them foregoes the advantage which comes from the experience of the race. They permeate the special functions which seem so separate, and bind them into a common plan and use. The organizing effect of such ideas helps one to escape that pseudo-education given by books of ten thousand facts, which is so attractive to scattered wits.

But with *knowledge*, with the *ideas*, the lad

will need certain established habits of mind that are *not* knowledge or ideas; such as Abraham Lincoln had, who must "bound" every important idea he would use, never at ease until he saw clearly what limited it on north, south, east, and west, with no borders lost in the mist. Such a habit is of use for any idea and for anybody. Because it is not the whole of reason we must not be blind to the part it can play in reason, immensely wide, even universal in its sweep. Then other habits are part of right intellectual equipment: controlled attention to the task in hand; energetic attack upon it; accuracy in interpreting, remembering and reporting what is seen or read or heard; the power to distinguish important and unimportant. These are part of intellectual training; these and other things take the place of the few faculties of the older belief. They stand out significant to an eye bewildered by the endless array of special functions which for some are the only things left. These wide and superior powers call for training, and the lad who has them trained has an incalculable advantage over every lad in whom they remain untrained.

There is cheer at this point for the teacher, the parent, discouraged by the child's talent for forgetting what has been painfully taught. Under the old creed which laid such stress upon memory, and even under the new with its stress upon "contents," there seems here but wasted effort. But we can now demonstrate experimentally that virtue may go into even the adept forgetter; power once developed remains even though upon the moment's examination the mind seems to have lost all its contents. Thomas Hanna, after a brain injury by a blow upon his head, lost all the detailed knowledge from both life and schooling; his "education" had in a certain sense been knocked out of him. And yet it remained, since he rapidly relearned what he had lost. So, too, the normal person, after disuse of the typewriter for years, so that nearly all the original skill seems gone, needs but a small part of the original practice to restore the whole. And the same seems to be true of poetry once learned and apparently quite forgotten. This is evidence that education goes deeper than memory and gives power that cannot be lost. The measure of accomplishment is now known to lie, not solely in what the child can recollect, but also in an imparted ability, temporarily become latent, but ready with little effort to be brought to full expression. This is a fact of cheer to weary workers.

V

EMOTION AND MENTAL ENERGY

But were we now to look to the *energy* of the mind, we should find something of wider bearing, evident not only in our thinking, but in every form of will. This energy makes itself known in the strength of the man's attention, in the vigor of his intellectual attack, and, out beyond intelligence, in his endurance, in the impact and tenacity of his purpose. Its amount is not the same as the amount available, which suffers changes not due merely to the ups and downs of health. Some crisis, as all know from James's essay on "The Energies of Men," may open a hidden reservoir from which power now flows into a man's every act. In the World War, men and women who had before been working to their utmost, suddenly assumed duties that trebled their task. The occasion, the solemn public demand, worked in them so that energy came forth to meet the need. No new function may have been called to life, but rather the long-familiar acts felt an access of energy — as an electric light, burning dull, suddenly receives fresh current, and leaps into brilliance. In this store of energy connected with all functions, whether they be special or general, we have an intimation of the mind as of another plan than has too often been taught. It is not a mere composite of general faculties, nor a composite of particular functions, but something single and yet varied, holding together all functions, and energizing them with a common life.

Now, if we were to ask as to the sources of energy, we should be led close to the emotions, where are found changes deep and wide that reveal new possibilities in education.

For the fruit of every one of our intellectual powers is markedly affected by the emotions behind them and interfused with them. There is a whole group of passions which in certain forms and intensities are strength-giving, are energetic —hope, for example, and gladness and anger: to these we should doubtless look for the cause of that opening of the gates of energy in crises when energy is our sorest need. They make and unmake the man. They hold our powers together; they disorganize and disrupt. The war brought new illustrations of this, where emotional stress and strain, without wounds, caused soldiers to be blind and deaf, unable to speak even their own names, great stretches of their past a blank to them. A like influence of emotion upon the total organization of the mind has long been observed in hysteria, with its functional blindness and deafness, its functional paralyses, its disturbance of memory and of the very feeling of one's identity. In all these cases something beneath the special functions has broken, and for the time their cunning is gone. Their life, then, is clearly not in themselves; in part at least it wells up from deeper sources.

But far short of these violent disturbances, we may see the emotions, the feelings, the moods, widely influencing the mind. The effect of emotion upon judgment is notorious: according as we like or dislike a person, will his acts be differently interpreted; according as we are elated or depressed will a task seem easily within or quite beyond our powers. For this reason children whose vitality is low cannot be expected to enter upon their work with normal interest and zeal. It seems probable that emotional depression hinders the power to recollect, and that recollection improves with a lifting of the emotional level. Strange to say, emotion even works *backward*, increasing or diminishing our power to recollect what occurred before, as well as during, the emotion itself. A knowledge of these interconnections makes for tolerance: the teacher's, the parent's own judgment is subject to fluctuations due to abundance or want of cheer. Health and buoyancy in the teacher, health and buoyancy in the taught, multiply the power available.

Some experiments in our laboratory have a bearing upon matters of the school, showing that surroundings clearly influence the power to learn. Students were set by Dr. Brown the task of solving a series of problems, working day after day, all at the same series of problems. Half of the youths worked one at a time in a room neatly carpeted, orderly, bright, and with a cheerful outlook. The other half were required to work one at a time in a room with bare floors, dingy, chaotic with odds and ends of apparatus, well lighted from above, but with no outlook. Those who had the pleasanter surroundings greatly outdistanced their competitors. It encourages us to think that schoolrooms, study-rooms at home, if made pleasant, give more than pleasure itself; they increase the work accomplished, the fruit of the effort. And in a different experiment the effect of the emotional attitude of the worker showed its effect. A score or more of youths had singly been set by Mrs. McCharles the same problems to solve; half of the workers were charged to regard each task as something well-disposed to them and to be met in as friendly a spirit as possible; the other half were to regard the work as an enemy that must be attacked with anger. The latter spirit, in a group of students otherwise not superior to their competitors, brought much larger success in the work. With animals in our laboratory it is found, by students under Dr. Tolman's direction, that a mild penalty attached to each mistake shortens the process of learning — an incentive more in favor with an older generation of schoolmasters, and which I here report "without recommendation." Nor would all be willing to imitate that similar use of the emotions as an aid to learning, reported by Benvenuto Cellini, when his father, showing him a salamander in their household fire, beat the lad lest he forget the rare experience.

Emotions never know their place; they wander and make strange transfers and associations. They appear in unexpected places. A young woman whom I know came near drowning upon a moonlit night some years ago; and now upon any night when the moon is bright the old distress in awakened form returns, there is an echo of the agony of her struggle. So far as this goes it tends to disturb and hinder the free expression of power. In a wider and beneficent way, we know that love may quicken the thought, the imagination, the purposes, of the lover; fresh life has pulsed through all his powers.

The play of emotion thus reveals the mind. If its powers seem stubbornly specialized and separate and insulated, this is true only in part and for the surface. Deep within we find free intercourse, free circulation. For all its particularized abilities, then, the mind is whole and fluid. A passion acts in it like a drop of strong chemical, that causes ebullition or precipitation throughout the whole. We cannot afford to neglect these universal potencies. The sect called Christian Scientists, with its eye upon some of these energizing emotions, shows that the neglect is being noted and avenged. And the growing attention to play is something of a belated redress. We once thought that health and mental vigor needed mere muscular contractions, so many foot-pounds of exercise *per diem*. The spirit of play in the exercise is the secret elixir, and with it apparently the exercise can almost be spared. Some day we shall know how much the great and balanced workers owe to their power to play—in mind if not in body. Wilson, like Lincoln, enjoyed the theater; and humor was a grace of each. With a right grasp of the mind's character the emotions will come into their own. They are not mere disturbers, mere ornaments; they decide whether the abilities shall be blocked or set free. Time and some impatience will bring us to share the conviction of the wise physician, Sir James Crichton-Browne, that in all education the emotions need uncommon care; that the right and sensitive emotions of the person can alone give effect to his learning and his judgment and his skill of hand.

VI

THE ORGANIZATION OF IMPULSES AND WILL

BUT the emotions are not alone in need of care. The impulses and the will cry out their own neglect. This is the more important, for they too lead us beyond the thought of independent functions and faculties, until we see the mind's worth as something decided largely by the quality of its organization, and we see, too, that this organization can be directed toward the better or the worse. The neglect and the opportunity here invite our full attention.

All children, if we look closely at their conduct, show a number of inborn traits — among others, an interest in possessing things, an attachment to other persons, a desire to shine in one's own and in others' eyes, a curiosity, a driving toward contention and domineering. And according as these native impulses, similar in all children and youths, are bound together in one or another way, there result men that stand opposite to one another like day and night. Let us take extremes to see the difference clear.

In one kind of youth these various impulses act almost in independence. Each pushes toward its goal with hardly a touch from the others; unchecked, the youth drives straight at what he would possess; when curious he prowls and pries without let or hindrance; now he is all affection and generosity, now he is wholly the bully and braggart.

In another youth these impulses are made the slaves of one of their roughest number. The interest in possessions, let us say, or in self-aggrandizement, has become a ruling passion; and if curiosity is still alive, it lives only to serve this master.

In still a third youth the impulses are strong and united, but in a freer way, keeping watch upon one another; no one of them can stir without ears pricked up in all the rest; and its behavior is subject to their urging and restraint. But our present youth is, indeed, a fortunate youth, for in him the sense of attachment to others, expanded and refined into obligation, speaks the last word to all the competing interests. Curiosity is free, the love of admiration, the love of property, is free, and is encouraged to fresh life; each may summon the rest to its assistance; but always this free life is within the wide bounds fixed by respect for other persons. Such a mind is not in chains; its love of distinction is not dead, neither is it inordinate; there is a desire to shine, but not at any cost or in any manner. Instead of vanity and the craving for notoriety (the rank growth of aggrandizement in fops and in some criminals), the love of admiration has been trained to fine strength. The native impulses have been brought to their place and proportion, each active, each tempered by its neighbors, each contributing to the right expression of the whole, each trained like the soldiers of the Tenth Legion both to command and to obey.

Such training is both private and social. The individual is enriched and also the community. For in a man so trained the instincts that either devastate or upbuild our common life, the instincts of pugnacity and of sex, have become not enemies, but friends of the general good. Disloyalty to this great interest, even that exceptional treachery which takes the form of crime, is usually from neglect or misguidance. Few, if any, men are born with truly ungovernable passions. The criminal is usually one in whom the right relation, the right organization, of his own deep promptings has been possible, but has never been attained. He has remained uneducated, even though his mind may have been filled with useful knowledge — used in his case for perverse ends.

It is thus evident that the mind is not a mere assembling of powers side by side; it is an organization of powers, some within others, some ruling others, using others as their instruments. There is a hierarchy of functions; and we must see to the regnant ones, making sure that the right impulsions rule, and that they are also made skillful and given concrete knowledge so that they may rule aright.

Now, the possibility and the need of care and organization of these deep impulses, called instincts, until they attain a right form of will, hardly appear in many a picture of the mind. Neither a group of independent faculties nor a group of independent functions reveals this constitution and opportunity. The mental disciplinarian, all eyes upon observation, memory, and reasoning, would strike into the depths of intellect, but misses those still lower depths of the affection, the instincts, and the will. Advocates of "contents" declare that the mind needs no care for its form and organization; it needs only to be filled. Such a mistake is not made by William James when he says that "there is reason to suppose that if we often flinch from making an effort, before we know it the effort-making capacity will be gone"; and that "the man who has daily inured himself to habits of concentrated attention, energetic volition, and self-denial in unnecessary things . . . will stand like a tower when everything rocks around him, and when his softer fellow-mortals are winnowed like chaff in the blast."

We might well regard the mind as inviting, and indeed requiring, not only particular training and useful information, but also a profound redirecting and strengthening of its inner order, not wholly unlike religious conversion. Such a change will usually not be sudden or marked by emotional storm, but gradually and in calm there will come a new perception and a new attachment of the affections and a striving toward a new goal. Something like this is in Plato's thought, that true education is that which leads us to love what we ought to love and to hate what we ought to hate from the beginning to the end.

Changes in the direction of the affections, even changes that seem instantaneous, are not confined to religion, but are general possibilities of our nature. A friend of mine, working ably in science, veered round to poetry, which thereafter remained his chief and lifelong interest. Another man, a successful merchant, was converted to learning, and selling all that he had, began years of further schooling. The interest which in such cases turns the man around has of course not been created on the instant; it was active all the while, but subordinate; and the conversion is but the final stage of a long struggle within. A new ordering of old interests and impulses has at last come, and a new stability is the result — as with an iceberg that by long melting below the ocean's surface must find a lost balance, and with a plunge shows to the air a new side.

Such changes with most of us, when they occur, are less cataclysmic, although no less real and profound. They are invited in early childhood and in the years when school and college are working in us good or ill. No system of education can afford to miss them and the constitution of the mind which they imply. The mind as we study it begins to reveal an immensity and an inner life hardly dreamt of by many who repeat solemnly what they take to be the final word of science. Each man's mind is doubtless as varied and deep and wide, in its own way, as is the physical world. Its soundings and its sweep will forever exceed description, yet we can already dimly discern some of the forces that bind and move and strain the whole, a view which does not contradict but corrects those who notice only what is local and minute.

VII

THE CARE OF THE EMOTIONS

BUT some, while admitting that the corrected account of the mind may be truer to the facts, will deny that it is important for education. We must forever go on storing the mind and exercising its separate functions or faculties, they would hold, not because this alone is good, but because this alone is possible. "How can we unlock the child's reservoir of energy?" they will ask; "How are we to make his emotions strength-givers indeed and not his ruin? Is it possible to enter among his wild instincts, leaving them no longer to howl in anarchy or under despotism, but to be a commonwealth governed freely by the best?"

It will require genius here as elsewhere to reveal fully what is admirable and fit for the work — genius that, when it comes, will make all that has gone before seem mere groping. Yet even now we can see something of the way along which we must go. Let me set down, almost as in a formal catalogue, particulars close to practice that promise to be of use in dealing with the emotions.

1. Emotions are of two kinds: strength-giving, *sthenic* emotions, like cheer, self-confidence, good-will, love; and the strength-taking, *asthenic* emotions, like fear, shame, gloom. Even the weakening emotions have their place and use; there are times when we should be checked in mid-career. Yet such emotions are good only by exception and for a short time. The strength-giving emotions are for long and steady use; they add impetus, they put driving force into the machinery of interest and purpose. These are the emotions of the child which we should strive to make enduring.

2. What shall be the dominant emotions of the child will depend in part upon the condition of his body: upon freedom from disease; upon suitable food; upon physical exercise, including work that is measured to his strength; and upon sufficient and regular sleep. There is a natural cheer in children; they normally will have the strength-giving emotions if the hindrances to such emotions are removed.

3. But much will count beside bodily condition. A teacher who is happy can hardly have unhappy pupils; an irritable teacher will hardly have them other than cheerless and perplexed. Children catch more than learning; they catch

the emotions of those about them. They are imitative; they feel, even when they cannot fathom, the good-will, the hope, the want of interest, the depression, of the teacher.

4. But besides example and imitation, there are ways to arouse admiration, confidence, cheer, and affection. Words of encouragement and appreciation, an occasional bit of merriment, a good-natured pleasantry even to drag from some disaffected one a smile, a zeal for the children and for their work — these, when added to the recognized teacher-abilities, help to give an undertone of joy in the work. Children's healthy admiration for the teacher, and honest pride in her person and power, is not to be despised. Stanley, when in darkest Africa, felt that he must look to his person and dress, even to hold his black followers. Trivial means may increase prestige and give a buoyant confidence that difficulties are superable, which adds to the power actually to overcome them.

5. There should be those externals that give a sense of pleasing order in the room without crowding and distraction; there should be simple and harmonious ornament by wall-tinting and pictures and flowers. Cheery lighting with a pleasant garden or wooded outlook may at times

coax interest away from studies, but it will in the end repay in added energy for the work.

6. Irresponsible enjoyment of fine things, enjoyment directly sought and without ulterior motive, is worth the having. Pictures, instrumental music, songs, poetry, stories, and plays, if beautiful, are their own excuse for being; and the child should be encouraged to enjoy them, without tricking him through them into learning. If children can be taught to sing with pleasure some melodies of Bach's (as I have seen it done by little children at Mrs. Hocking's school at Cambridge), I should prefer to leave it unknown to them who Bach was or when or where he lived or any other fact of him or his music that the children unprompted did not care to know. Where fine appreciation is forever subordinated to the art of wedging knowledge into the mind, a large end is defeated. We must multiply and keep open the channels of right pleasure, of right appreciation, as having an equal place with knowledge.

7. Imagination and courtesies are a means to heighten sympathy and pleasure. Only by imagination can one see through the opaque covering of many a stranger, into the life beneath. Fairy tales are an early way to know that appear-

ance may belie reality, that the hunchback may be a prince in disguise, the toad an enchanted maiden. Imaginative stories supplement acquaintance, giving pleasure from unaccustomed goodness and evil, showing without disastrous experience the right opportunities for fear and confidence, for love and hate. Manners, courtesies, are also a stimulant to appreciation, as symbols of respect and good-will. While they may be but empty insincerity, they will normally suggest the value of others and will soften the asperities of self-interest which youth is apt to show.

8. The fine arts should be attempted and prized for their hidden effect within the child, and far less or not at all for some external product delightful to observers. Moreover, in plays or in dramatic singing, besides the delight of the children in the immediate performance, and the taste which will open to them new delights, something may be expected from assigning the parts so as *not* to give the most admirable result to the audience. I mean that while a blithe girl might more skillfully take a happy rôle, yet it would be shrewd to give the part to one who needs the gayety, letting some one well grounded in happiness play at solemnity or gloom. Those especially should try to sing who have no promise of voice, those paint

who never will be able to paint. Youthful attempts at the violin and sketching which come to nothing, I can testify, may make music and landscape constant sources of delight. Not, then, by their fruits visible to others are these childhood practices to be judged, but by what they leave behind concealed in the permanent springs of appreciation.

9. Emotions, if they are to be steady strengtheners of the mind, must become silent habits of emotion. An emotion is of little service that is a passing ebullition; it must become a durable trend, a lasting sentiment. Only occasionally will a situation arise that needs a passionate outpouring, fire and fury or ecstasy. And as for habits of emotion, they are knit up with habits of emotional expression, with habits of smiling, laughing, frowning, pouting, and the like. To attack or to build stronger the emotion-habit, one may well attack or fortify the emotional expression, making the scowler stop scowling, making the pout give way to a smile, even though it be at first galvanic. Youths and adults, even teachers, may gain by some suggestion to themselves of the feeling that should be there. They will learn, too, that in choosing one's associates — of persons, books, plays, or music — one is choosing

also in some degree the hue of his own feeling. Persons inclined to melancholy will hardly profit by books or friends that hang the heavens with black. Teachers should occasionally read Leacock and Lamb and Uncle Remus, and leave to the humorists the works of Schopenhauer and the whole tribe of the prophets of despair.

VIII

INSTINCTS WILD AND TAME

BUT the emotions cannot be separated from the instincts, nor these from the will. All are distinctions within the total life, and if the full mind is to be made effective, we must sketch some plan of action that drives hard into the realm of purpose. Can something here be suggested for those bent upon deeds and weary of theory and discussion? A few things should perhaps be set down.

1. To train the child's will we must have in it the great natural driving forces, but have these made beneficent. Each of the great native desires or impulses which we already have considered — the impulse to have property, to shine before others and to lord it over them, to feel their power and to humble ourselves before them, to quarrel, to love wife or husband, to love child, parent, and friend — each of these great forces is needed for its energy. Nor is each a rigid and intractable thing; it can be modified, can be educated, and through it the others can be reached. Indeed, each becomes safe and civil only by binding it into a system with the others, having them check and subdue it, compelling it to have outlet

and expression only with them. Let us consider some of these great impulses and see how the desired end is to be reached.

2. The passion for having and collecting things can be carried up into a love of great possessions. Birds' eggs, butterflies, minerals, and endless other things, may, with youths too solitary or self-centered, be made a way of entrance into companionship with those interested in like objects, and into sharing with new-found friends; with others, in whom taste or precise observation would be increased, they can be made to lead into drawing, painting, and literary description; with the joyless and all others, into an interested pleasure in the places and setting of the collected objects, a pleasure in trees, streams, mountains, and all nature that cannot be collected or appropriated. Starting as a narrow eagerness—a sheer cupidity, a passion to grasp and make many things *mine* and to exclude others from them—this greed is led on until it finds itself a delight freed from this exclusiveness, a delight in what is beautiful or wild, a delight in conversation, in friendship, in goods that are not subject to greed and amassing. Those who would civilize the possessive and commercial passion early can here find opportunity.

3. Self-appreciation, the desire to win admiration, must keep its strength and be disciplined into right ambition. In its early form it is a crude love of attention, and it may, if continued, become an itch for notoriety of any kind. But it need not remain base. It can be a wholesome satisfaction in one's own physical strength, and then a pleasure in one's will rather than strength, thence passing to skill of mind valued above deftness, until satisfaction is chiefly in the finer uses to which such spiritual skill can be put. This, when attained, delights to add to the things that are prized lastingly, and the early vanity of ambition has disappeared. Gladstone, we are told by John Morley, urged the students of Edinburgh to seek distinction, to gain reputation through true excellence. The power of ambition is thus used without its sting.

4. Self-abasement and pugnacity must also be there, trained into loyalty. The child's sense of insufficiency, of the masterful importance of others, which early appears as bashfulness before elders, and as "tagging after" those whose station is less imposing, may be guided into fealty. Boys find their heroes in men of strength and skill; in wrestlers, football captains, and mighty hunters. Samson, young David, Achilles, Liv-

ingstone, the hunter Roosevelt, rightly win the youth's attachment. But from prowess the admiring look can be reserved for the one who fights a good fight. The search for some one that can enlist the affections thus grows into a search for a cause worthy of one's full devotion and fighting strength, a cause that with time can almost be personified into the captain of one's soul. Attachment can join hands with fine jealousy and pugnacity, and the youth finds himself a volunteer against vice, against ignorance and disease, against human wastage in mines and factories, or against war; a volunteer in the fight for the welfare of children and women, for sanitation, for education, for social and political reform, for international order and organization. These great ardors, where one forgets himself and emembers only the great enterprise, are in childhood petty enough; and yet the petty forms are to be respected for what comes of them.

5. With regard to the sex impulse, more is needed than to satisfy curiosity, good as this may be. This imperious motive strikes into far more than intellect and questioning; it colors and forms imagination, emotion, sentiment, impulse, choice, and purpose. What becomes of this passion decides whether the character shall

be stable and upright or be out of plumb, resting on cracked foundations. Taboo is bad; but bad is it also to leave sex to physiology and hygiene. The whole mind must give it a right place, faced against giggling and prying, against the reading and pictures and conversation that stir and degrade, welcoming instead a loyal interest and a chivalry toward those of another sex. The high expectations which men have for women, and women for men, are the expression of this spirit; in such forms as these the troublesome impulse has become of right effect. The sex interest cannot be killed by free feeding; hope lies only in control, without fear, and in a free strength given to other interests. To resent coarseness in others helps to free one's self. Examples of such resentment in fine characters here will help. Colonel Newcome leaving the room in hot indignation when that old reprobate, Captain Costigan, sang a lewd song; that other colonel without fear, Theodore Roosevelt, rebuking a group of his men-hosts in the Northwest, telling them then and there, before all, that to his mind motherhood was not a subject for jest — these will help boys to avoid timid submission to what is gross, will elevate their interests and give courage.

6. The kindly attachments which run between

parent and child, brother and brother, friend and friend, need to come into wide good-will. The circle of affection which at first is narrowed to family and close companions must be widened to include in the mild yet strong sentiment of friendliness what is below, far out at one's own level, and above. The fabric of society comes from this quiet activity. Here, too, imagination enriched by acquaintance and by indirect experience through the reading of novels, biography, history, and poetry, may be joined with some overt suggestion, by teacher and parent, of what is hidden in the stranger. Pets, also, are educators of the affections and are occasions of angry defense, which is also a healthy expression of good-will.

7. These lacks in the passions show how far we must be carried beyond the regions of usual schooling and intelligence. No tests as yet strike in here. The talented youth who comes to naught; the unbrilliant youth who comes to great achievement; the apathetic child; the timid child, of "broken will"; — these and a host of other incompletions reveal how much is needed in education besides what is commonly included either in mental discipline or in information. Education must deal solidly with the sources of the mind's power, in emotion and will.

IX

EXERCISES FOR THE WILL

WITH this glance at the savage instincts become civilized, one may well turn to the will, ask what a strong will really is, and by what forging it has its temper.

1. And first we shall see that there are three features in a will that is trained, and that we must not think too exclusively of its sheer force. Violent, stormy children and adults have ample force, yet with wills undisciplined. An effective will has *vigor;* but, besides, it has *steadiness;* and, still more, *rightness of aim.* The will is not schooled until it has been brought to right measure in all these three respects, so that it is at once forcible, unswerving, and aimed a little above the very center of the target.

2. Steadiness has ten times the worth of sheer weight of blow. A friend of mine, a mere child, standing on the dock at Lake Tahoe, and leaning against a vessel there, gradually and without knowing it pushed the vessel away until she fell into the water. Had she rushed against the craft, she might have dashed herself to pieces

without budging it. So with the mind; the child's will is the wind's will, at first gusty and variable, until it can blow true, like the trades. Steadiness not only has ten times the effect of violence, it is ten times more readily attained. We can expect by training to make the will constant, where we can do little to alter its original force of attack. Let us then carry our admiration from the strong to the constant will. "It's dogged as does it!"

3. Steadiness of will means power to do the irksome, to resist the lure of the easy and the comfortable. The child must be psychically toughened, ready to defy his present sensations. Spartan youths were taught to stand pain. Their Athenian critic said that they and all other lads had better be taught to *stand pleasure* where character so often breaks down. This does not mean that there is no need to enlarge the circle of the agreeable; or that, with Mr. Dooley, it does not matter what you study so long as you hate it. More tasks can be made pleasant, but there will remain many unpleasant tasks that should not be avoided. The world will soon enough assign work which will be distasteful and must for success be labored into and through. Young Grenfell taking to the North Sea and then to Labrador, young Lincoln training himself where

all was uninviting — such men show the spare sinews of the will contemptuous of the merely pleasant.

4. Within reason, a decision once made should be held to tooth and nail. It may be that the purpose should be changed, but there should be prejudice against this. In general we can trust a child to adjust his will to new evidence, new experience, new opportunities; we can less securely trust him to escape the loss from that common trick of the mind by which upon committing one's self to a course, whatever it be, that course comes to seem rough and sunless. The vacillation which results is wasteful from the start, and grows to a habit of dropping things hardly begun. Children in whom this fickleness is not trained out, grow into men and women forever remodeling their houses before they are half-built.

5. Interruptions will occur; the will must swing back to its old direction, like a compass needle when the obstruction goes. Steadiness of will can in practice never mean an unbroken advance to the goal. It means a forgetting of the break, a homing again and again. Exercises could and should be conceived to bring the child spontaneously and of habit back to the unfinished work, to keep active in his subconsciousness the

old interest, ready to stand forth and summon him back to what is incomplete. Discouragement because of interruption is disastrous and avoidable; it should be forestalled by becoming expectant of breaks, and prepared to meet them on their own ground.

6. Will depends upon habits of muscular action and of thinking, along with habits of feeling and emotion. An effective will requires the support of an organized group of habits, habits of hand, of speech, of weighing and deciding, of steady attachments and aversions, in a thousand forms and directions. Will has built into it habits; and unless they be for us they will be against us. No one can conquer who has not an army of such helpers that can be depended upon — no more than can a general, a genius in strategy, but without troops.

7. There must be a right direction of the will. It is not enough that the will be powerful and unswerving. The hunter of steady aim must aim at the right thing; and not, as did one in the Sierra, who wounded a friend of mine, mistaking him for a bear! Napoleon, Bismarck, of almost irresistible purpose, lacked some powerful ingredient to complete their will. The defect is not so much a failure to see the facts, as a failure to appraise the

facts seen; a true scale of valuation is lacking. Until this is supplied by an imparting of taste, morals, and religion, the will has only a form of training, and lacks substance. Without wisdom, then, the will is a powerful instrument whose effect is all insecure. Guidance must enter into the constitution of will; its impulses must be subject to a love of the Best.

8. The desired qualities of will should be sought not alone by maxim, encouragement, and command; *graded exercises* there should be, suited to the age of the child. Parents and teachers might well invent and assign things to be done, rewarding in themselves, and chosen, perhaps, from cooking, drawing, modeling, painting, acting, reading, or any other of a hundred things — but now used in order to make habitual the right ways of purpose, applicable in any work. These right ways might here be set down, with another purpose than was guiding us earlier in this section, as: (*a*) suitable forethought; (*b*) speed and energy of attack, once the decision is made; (*c*) perseverance in what is undertaken; (*d*) economy of action, elimination of waste effort, "form"; (*e*) excellence of result in the product; (*f*) restoration of order when the work is done, putting away of tools and materials, clearing and clean-

ing up. Each of these six phases of the process should receive due attention, — perhaps one at a time, as Benjamin Franklin practiced the virtues, — but recurring, and with different degrees of difficulty. There should be brief explanation before and after the fact, that the *idea* of what is sought should come with the practice, and should help to make the practice itself more fruitful and ready to reappear spontaneously in new places. And whatever is approved elsewhere as a means to interest and progress might be used here; if "marks," rewards, praise, or rivalries are good to spur on in numbering or writing or any other study, this present learning to will aright is as worthy of their incentive.

9. As an exercise in suitable forethought, the following might serve as a door to something better. There is, let us say, but ten minutes left, and the child must choose between cutting some design in paper and making candy; and the choice is then appraised, with explanation, according as the child has stopped to think, to look ahead, before deciding. Or, again, having at hand only some modeling wax, a pair of scissors, and some very narrow strips of thin colored paper, one must decide whether to build a paper house or make the figure of a dog. Or still again, the

child, without actual materials at hand and with the use only of his imagination, must say — with no change of vote permitted — which line of conduct is suitable, either in cases like those just given, or where some one of a thousand other situations is described — where, perhaps, a child has visiting playmates who have come walking from afar and up a long steep hill; shall they at first play "authors" or play "tag"?

10. For an exercise in persistence, the child, having started upon something which he himself, perhaps, has chosen, is "marked," is praised or left unpraised, according to the full constancy with which he continues to its end the work in hand. For the earlier and easier steps in such an exercise, that can be matched in its duration and in all else to the child's years and progress, there will be an absence of intentional distraction and temptation that must be resisted; there will be enough to contend with in the spontaneous prompting to slow up, to stop, to do something else. But when self-control has reached its proper pitch, the set task will be to continue without remission when things lie at hand to play with, or when the other children are at attractive work or at play. If it is known beforehand to be a trial of constancy, joyously announced as a

chance to show the stuff one is made of, with praise and reward waiting on success, the child can delight to stand the test, as a young Redskin schooled and glad to endure pain. Good workers often seem to need something to struggle against, some challenge that wakes and nerves them to put their muscles and brain in fighting trim. With fuller mastery there must also be actual interruptions, with free return to the work as soon as possible. Power to remember and re-attack work broken into is central to all excellence.

11. It is clear that a will fully trained is in truth a character trained. It is an organization of many, indeed all, of our different impulses, native and acquired, colored by all our conscious interests and affections, colored and guided by experience and knowledge and formulated principles of action. All the parts and forces of will should come within our planning, should be dealt with by a system that draws from the imagination and from the findings of careful experiment. Many and great are the trained will's requirements: to be intelligent, escaping at once the missteps that come from stupidity and from inexperience; to be self-reliant, yet receiving the help of others which no one can forego; to be a seeker of possessions, but mainly of the kind that

no one can steal; to be cheerful and of good-will; to have conscience lit with knowledge. The teacher's task is thus to remake the child entire, to make of him a person; it is, to use Stevenson's words, a task for all that a man has of fortitude and delicacy.

The task is, indeed, difficult and demands the talent of creative artists. Not in one generation nor in two will the means be discovered and brought to bear. But whatever comes of the best family life or of fortunate friendships or of great public opportunity and need — whatever comes to the mind's benefit from these is clearly within the aim of right education. Whatever can be wrought by happy environment can in some measure be wrought by the school, which is an environment planned and chosen. The result may be of less amount than comes from beyond school, but it need have no different quality. And most of all where the world beyond school promises the child not the best, but only the worst family life, with no fortunate friendships and only the bleak prospect of factory and mill and mine, then is the demand insistent that we neglect nothing that will even slightly remake the mind into what is right and whole. Men persevered at aviation from the days of Dædalus, closing their ears to the wagging gray-beards who cried "impossible." An honored professor of mine, a physicist of distinction, used to demonstrate to us that the attempt to make a flying machine was absurd; even as others had proved that slavery was part of the eternal ordinance of God. But once recognize the demand, and the inventive will of man is indomitable. So in education we shall have faith in things to come; we shall welcome all manner of experimental schools, especially those which look steadily to true understanding and to the will and the affections, out of which are the issues of life. Effectively to love what ought to be loved and to hate what ought to be hated requires, not heart alone, but brain and hand and tongue.

X

ESTABLISHING GOVERNMENT IN THE MIND

THE education that is needed will touch the person, part and entire, body and spirit, running through senses, memory, understanding, affections, and will. It will not frown upon special activities; they are facts which, if neglected by any plan, will grind it to powder. The school, then, will take particular functions in hand, practicing them to do their work. There will be no reluctance to give substantial knowledge to the child, without which his action will be blind. But going beyond the empty exercise of intellectual powers, while valuing them and the knowledge that should be had, it will, above all, look to the total organization, the foundation, the great stresses and strains in the structure of the person.

The relation of this to the rival assertions which were early examined and found disappointing, is perhaps thus entirely clear; but it may be illustrated from the human body which, with all its separate organs and special functions, must attain a unity which is not there from the beginning, so that ear serves eye, eye hand, hand lips.

The interrelations of these members are multiplied and strengthened; they are stirred and controlled by hidden glands, by nerves, by brain that is both servant and master of them all. Powers are present which no one of us can outright create, but by taking thought we extend, contract, and modify them into harmony and fuller coöperation.

So it must be with the whole person. His total nature must not escape us, lost in particulars. The child is a living system of many powers, powers not side by side, indifferent, mosaic-like. He cannot be taken and educated piecemeal. The forces that drive through his whole being, that make or unmake him, must never be lost to view.

It will be clear that there is no special virtue in doing what is intrinsically useless, although poetry may be as useful as typewriting. But the sinews of the mind can strengthen on what is of service and delight, of which there is enough, without incessant treadmill work. Better to paint the ship, for discipline, than to knock rust off the anchor.

There is, in the view here attained, aid and comfort for those who would interconnect the different sides of schooling, making each interest of the child, each subject studied, enrich and kindle the rest: making literature add to history and geometry, and receive from them; while music and drawing and acting inspire them all. Going thus far, one can go farther, contriving subjects and situations and exercises that do not scatter, but unite, bringing the child's interests into more perfect order, making his will to be of steady and wise power. In all this we must hold fast to the good, while hospitable toward the untried.

When we are offered a new lamp for an old, we must rub the new to see how much of the old Aladdin magic it contains. Let us have the new with the least loss. The cry for special training is a cry also for specialists as teachers; and desirable as they are, they will bear watching; for in choosing them, the temptation will be to ask only what and how much they know. And, as in the new proposal the child is almost forgotten for the things he is to learn, so the stuff of the teacher can too easily disappear behind the bales of information he offers. Moreover, with specialists it is touch-and-go with their pupils. In the great city schools there is little of the leisurely contact, little of the intimacy, without which the imparting of useful knowledge is as sounding brass. The archaic teacher who taught the same children everything that lay between Shakespeare and the rings of Saturn, at least became acquainted with his pupils, and little in him escaped their ferret eyes. Factory methods may be excellent for highly specialized mental functions, but not for the whole strong structure of the mind. Upbuilding can come only from those that have it, and the demand for it must not weaken in the demand for the expert in his field. An erect mind knowing the salient things will do more to quicken and give a right facing to other minds than will a dozen husks of humanity with the entire alphabet in capitals after their names.

Instead, then, of following whole-heartedly the new lights of education whose gospel is that subjects are more important than minds, we shall reaffirm the exact opposite while yet opening the door to the useful. The child is bigger than anything he can carry to market. In him is a divinity ready for employment, but greater than any employment that he will choose. In fitting the child to his job, we must have a live child left. This means no slighting of details. His general powers must be brought down to particulars, and to particulars that are useful. His thinking will not be counted as trained until he can demonstrate, not only some proposition in geometry, but the truths that touch children, women, and men, that touch the life of farm and city, that touch international security.

If the child be more than his information, we shall not neglect his taste. He will be sensitive to beauty, but by some toughening of his fiber he will escape daintiness and a repugnance to what is wholesome and of the soil. He will know the way into the enchanted world of music and painting and literature, but with a strengthened grasp of common duty; he will not treat lightly what he owes to family and friend and to plain man everywhere.

And he will have reverence. This great completion may not aid him as a producer of commodities; it may even hinder. But as Dr. Cabot has reminded us that some of the greatest things of life are unhygienic, so we shall not forget that some are uneconomic. Man, as was said of old, is indeed the great amphibian. He suffocates if kept from the upper air. There must be intercourse with uses great and small, but also with that great world which passes judgment upon all use.

No symbol does justice to the mysterious relation between the mind and him who helps it to its power. The teacher is like a physician, assisting at the birth of the mind, the mind which before exists all cramped, not breathing as yet. But he also feeds the mind, he guides its first steps, he gives it gymnastics, he gives toys and tools. He is the mind's autocrat, but an autocrat who knows when revolution is due, and abdicates; so wise that he has provided against anarchy, has trained many for office, and has trained others to recognize them, so that self-government moves quietly into the departed ruler's place.

No symbol is adequate, but should we not be shrewd bargainers if we exchanged both the image of the stripped athlete with Indian clubs, and the image of the tool-chest well stocked, for the figure of a city-state with its inhabitants becoming trained to artisan tasks, trained to build and enjoy parks and museums, theaters and sanctuaries; trained also to enter and to respect the massive halls of justice and law-making and command? At home in all these broad spaces, he who is bringing into order the great city pauses here for a moment and encourages, passes on and sits down and patiently guides; and in the end, and with many helpers different from himself and with a favoring fortune, the republic of the mind is established and unfurls its splendid banner with festival and song.

OUTLINE

I. IS THE MIND A GYMNASIUM OR A TOOL-CHEST?

II. DEFECTS IN THE RIVAL ACCOUNTS

III. THE INTERPLAY OF MIND AND BODY

IV. INFLUENCES WITHIN INTELLIGENCE

V. EMOTION AND MENTAL ENERGY

VI. THE ORGANIZATION OF IMPULSES AND WILL

IX. EXERCISES FOR THE WILL

X. ESTABLISHING GOVERNMENT IN THE MIND

OUTLINE